Jesus Worked Miracles

For my mom,
who first taught me
to believe in Christ.
—Heidi

ISBN 13: 978-1-4621-3991-0

Published by CFI, an imprint of Cedar Fort, Inc.
2373 W. 700 S., Springville, UT 84663
Distributed by Cedar Fort, Inc., www.cedarfort.com

Cover design and typesetting by Shawnda T. Craig

Edited by Abby Fales

Printed in the United States of America

10 9 8 7 6 5 4 3 2 1

Printed on acid-free paper

Jesus Worked Miracles

Written by Heidi Poelman • Illustrated by Jason Pruett

CFI • An imprint of Cedar Fort, Inc. • Springville, Utah

As the Son of God

and Creator of the earth,

Jesus can do anything.

His first miracle was small. A wedding party had run out of wine for their guests. His mother wondered if Jesus could help.

Jesus asked for several pots of water. He turned the water into wine. After that, people knew Jesus was different.

A wealthy man saw what Jesus had done. He came to Jesus and asked if He would heal his sick son.

Jesus replied,
"Go thy way; thy son liveth."
(John 4:48-50)

The man hurried toward home. When he was nearly there, his servants came out shouting that his son's fever had gone!

Happily, the father asked when his son had recovered. The servants replied, "Yesterday at the seventh hour."

(John 4:52)

The man was amazed! It was the same time that Jesus had said all would be well. The whole household knew Jesus was special.

Believers began seeking Jesus. A leper with terrible sores came to Him. The man said, "Lord, if thou wilt, thou canst make me clean."

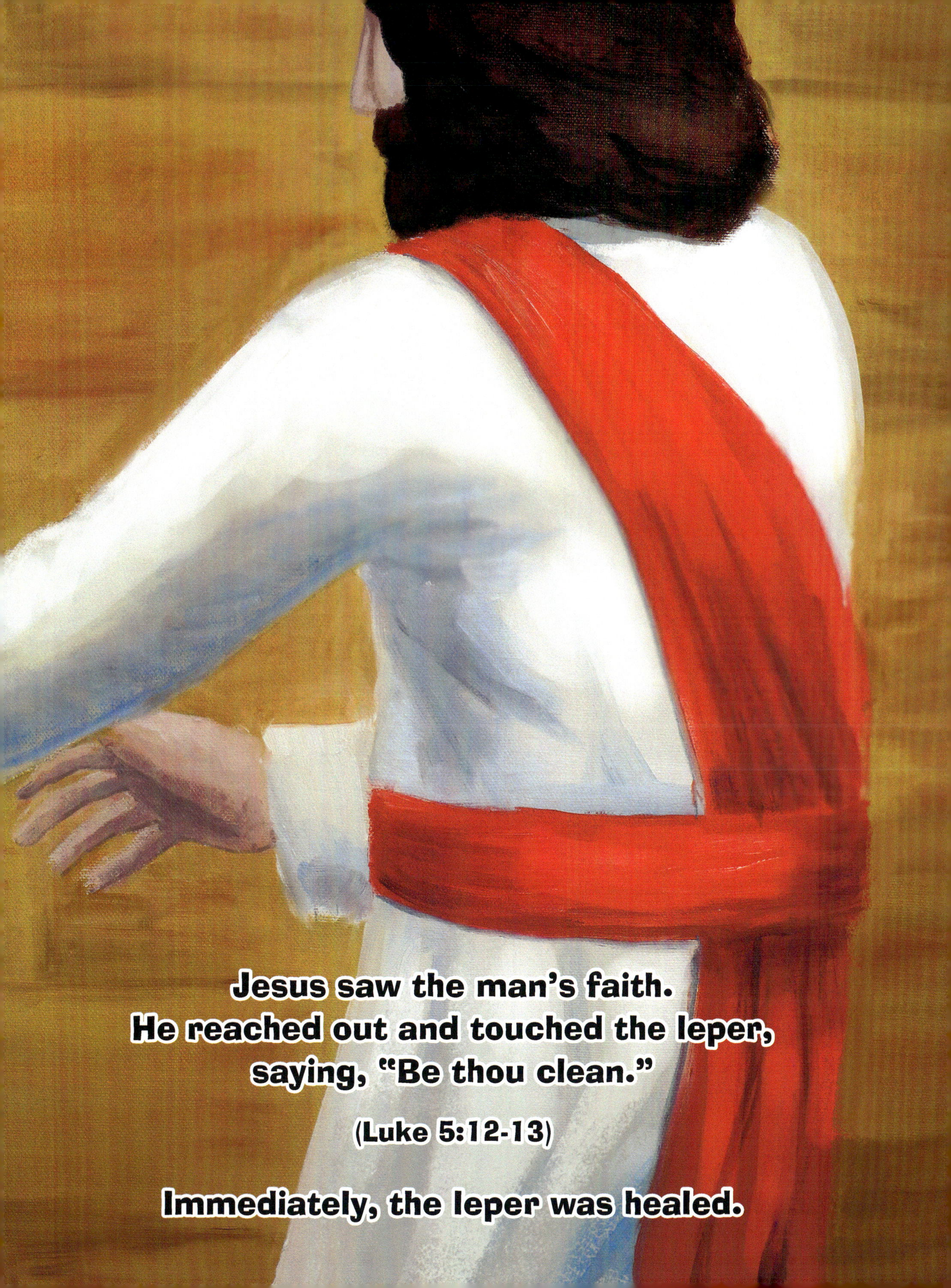

Jesus saw the man's faith.
He reached out and touched the leper,
saying, "Be thou clean."

(Luke 5:12-13)

Immediately, the leper was healed.

Jesus chose 12 disciples to help Him teach the people. They were on a ship when a storm came. The winds were strong and the waves were big, but Jesus slept quietly.

Afraid, the disciples woke Jesus. He stood and said to the sea, "Peace, be still."

(Mark 4:38-39)

Suddenly, the waters were calm.

Jesus was teaching one day when more than 5,000 people started to follow Him. It was already late in the day. The people were hungry, but they wanted to stay and listen. All the group had to eat was five loaves of bread and two fishes. The disciples asked Jesus what they should do.

Jesus asked to hold the bread and fishes. He blessed them, broke them into pieces, and passed them to the crowd. The disciples watched as every single person was fed. Later, Jesus taught, "I am the bread of life: he that cometh to me shall never hunger."

(John 6:35)

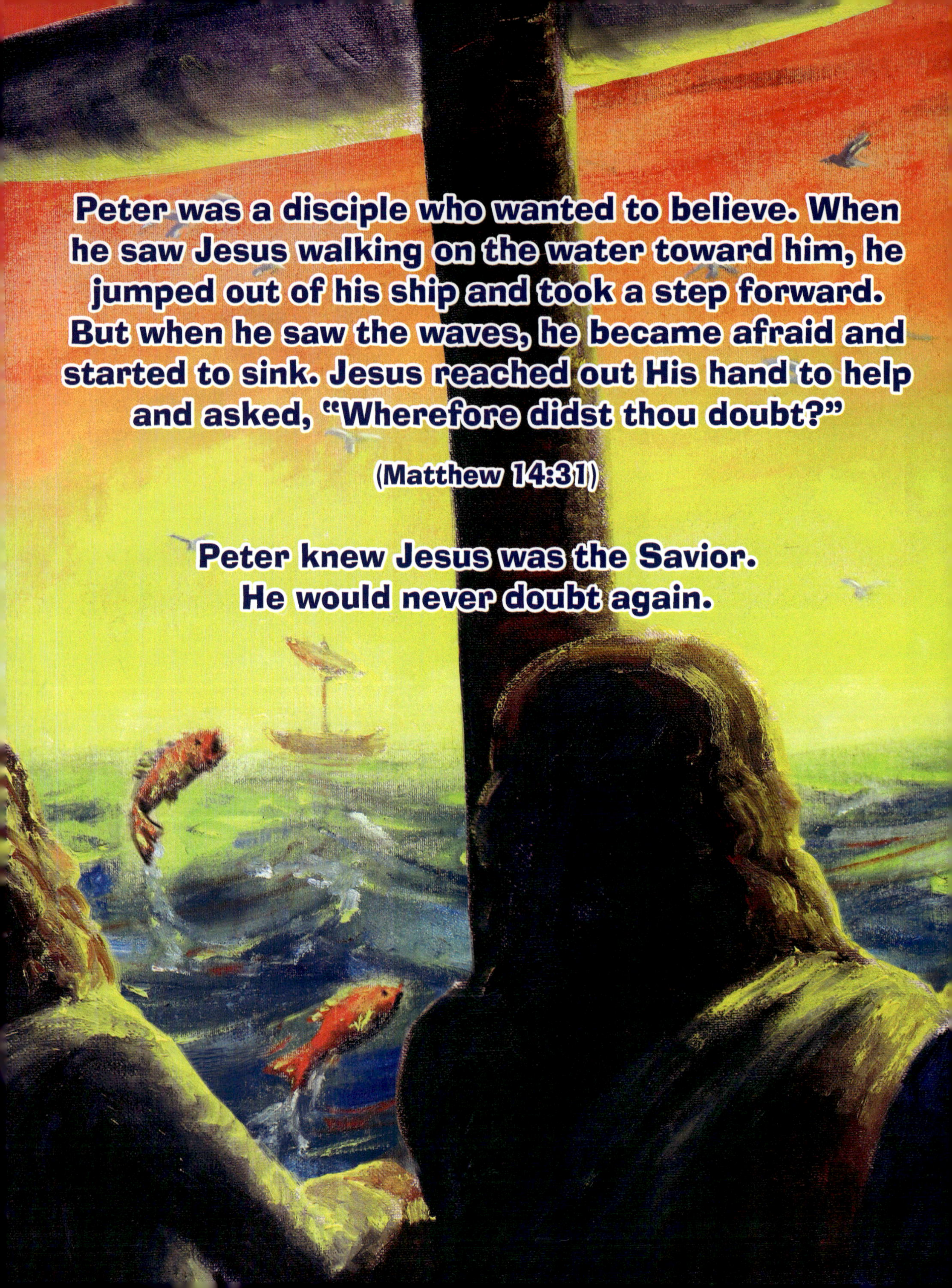

Peter was a disciple who wanted to believe. When he saw Jesus walking on the water toward him, he jumped out of his ship and took a step forward. But when he saw the waves, he became afraid and started to sink. Jesus reached out His hand to help and asked, "Wherefore didst thou doubt?"

(Matthew 14:31)

Peter knew Jesus was the Savior.
He would never doubt again.

Jesus went on to help and heal many more people.

The blind He caused to see. The lame He caused to walk. The sinners He made clean. He told them, "If ye have faith . . . nothing shall be impossible unto you."

(Matthew 17:20)

One day, Jesus found out that His good friend Lazarus had died. Jesus wept for His lost friend. Then He said to Lazarus's family, "He that believeth in me, though he were dead, yet shall he live."

(John 11:25)

The Savior walked to the tomb. Four days had passed since Lazarus had died. Jesus asked someone to roll away the stone that blocked the opening. Then He stood outside and called, "Lazarus, come forth."

(John 11:43)

Lazarus rose and walked out of the tomb! This time, the believers knew Jesus could do anything. That made some people angry.

Leaders of the land decided to put Jesus to death. As He hung from the cross, Jesus wasn't angry. He prayed, saying, "Father, forgive them; for they know not what they do."

(Luke 23:34)

After Jesus died, believers laid His body in a tomb. Many people were sad. They thought this was the end.

But it wasn't the end at all!

On the third day, Jesus rose and walked out of His tomb. Death could not conquer the Savior. It was His greatest miracle of all.

In overcoming death, Jesus gave us all the gift of eternal life. Now, we can be comforted during our storms. We can be healed when we are hurting. And when our loved ones die, we know we can see them again someday.

Jesus works miracles still for all those who believe.

"I am the light of the world: he that
followeth me shall not walk in darkness,
but shall have the light of life."
(John 8:12)